CONTENTS

KU-863-410

IT'S ALL ABOUT YOU

Fill in all your important information here! Then if your book gets lost, whoever finds it will know where to return it.

Stick your photo here.

Name: _____

Nickname: _____

Age: _____

Address: _____

School: _____

Form: _____

Teacher: _____

Draw what you wear to school on this boy.

What You Wear To School

What colour is your school uniform?

_____

Do you have to wear a tie?

_____

Do you have to wear a blazer?

_____

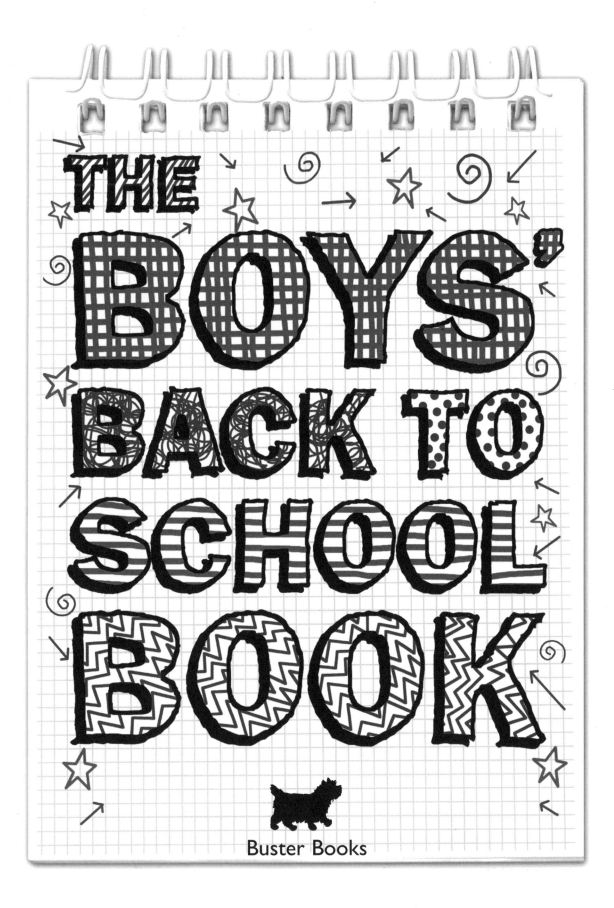

THE BOYS' BACK TO SCHOOL BOOK

Buster Books

Written by Steve Martin
Illustrated by Paul Moran
Edited by Jaine Keskeys
Cover by Becky Chilcott
Designed by Barbara Ward

First published in Great Britain in 2011 by Buster Books, an imprint of Michael O'Mara Books Limited, 9 Lion Yard, Tremadoc Road, London SW4 7NQ

A CIP catalogue record for this book is available from the British Library.

ISBN: 978-1-907151-50-7

2 4 6 8 10 9 7 5 3 1

www.mombooks.com/busterbooks

This book was printed in May 2011 at L.E.G.O., Viale dell'Industria 2, 36100, Vicenza, Italy.

READY FOR ANYTHING

It's amazing how much stuff you need for a new year at school. A bit of planning can stop you being caught out. Nobody wants to arrive at school and find they've forgotten their PE kit or, worse still, their lunch!

First, complete the list of things you think you'll need. Then tick the boxes to show how ready you are.

Essential equipment	Already have	Still need to get	Essential equipment	Already have	Still need to get
School bag					
Pencil case					
Ruler					
Pen for writing					
Felt-tip pens					
Pencil					
Eraser					
Pencil sharpener					
Maths set					
Lunchbox					

Top Tip!

Ask yourself these questions. What will I need to wear? What will I need to do my work? Do I need food, drink or money to buy them? Is there something I want to show my friends?

ARE YOU THE HISTORY KING?

The problem with history is that there's just so much of it! Find out how much you and your friends know about the last 2,000 years. Put each player's answers (A, B, C or D) on the scorecard and then check the answers on page 62.

1. Which ancient language did the Romans speak?

A. French
B. Latin
C. English
D. Greek

2. Who built the Pyramids?

A. The Egyptians
B. The Druids
C. The Greeks
D. The Vikings

3. Who was the first European to discover Australia?

A. Captain Cook
B. Captain Chef
C. Captain Baker
D. Captain Butcher

4. Who was the first president of the USA?

A. Abraham Lincoln
B. Ronald Reagan
C. Barack Obama
D. George Washington

5. During the French Revolution, what was the guillotine used for?

A. Cutting bread
B. Cutting hair
C. Cutting people's heads off
D. Cutting paper to the right size

6. In which part of the world would you have found the great Aztec civilization?

A. Central America
B. Northern Europe
C. South Africa
D. The West Indies

7. The terrible plague that killed millions of Europeans in the 14th century is called the ...

A. Red Death
B. Black Death
C. Grey Death
D. Purple Death

8. Which of the following was invented first?

A. The car
B. The train
C. The computer
D. The television

9. Who was the first man to set foot on the moon?

A. Lance Armstrong
B. Buzz Aldrin
C. Neil Armstong
D. Buzz Lightyear

11. How many wives did the King Henry VIII of England have?

A. 3
B. 4
C. 5
D. 6

10. Who was the Prime Minister of the United Kingdom during World War II?

A. Benjamin Disraeli
B. William Gladstone
C. Margaret Thatcher
D. Winston Churchill

12. How long is the Great Wall of China?

A. 50 km
B. 1,000 km
C. 8,850 km
D. 20,500 km

Question	Player 1	Player 2	Player 3	Player 4
1				
2				
3				
4				
5				
6				
7				
8				
9				
10				
11				
12				
Total				

DESIGN YOUR OWN SHIELD

In medieval times, families designed their own coats of arms. Knights would then display these on their shields, so that their comrades knew who they were. Choosing shapes and pictures for a coat of arms is called 'heraldry'.

Use the shield below to design your own coat of arms.

YOUR FAVOURITE SUBJECT

Everybody has their own idea about the best subjects at school.
Fill in the sheet below, answering the questions about your
favourite subject and then ask two friends to do the same.

Me	Friend 1	Friend 2
Name	Name	Name
Favourite school subject	Favourite school subject	Favourite school subject
What I like most about this subject	What I like most about this subject	What I like most about this subject
Three things I have learned in this subject	Three things I have learned in this subject	Three things I have learned in this subject
1.	1.	1.
2.	2.	2.
3.	3.	3.
A job I could do related to this subject	A job I could do related to this subject	A job I could do related to this subject

EXTREME SPORTS LESSON

Brilliant! It's time for your PE lesson, so grab your kit
and solve these sporty puzzles. Check your answers on page 62.

Get Ready For Games

A   B   C   D   E   F

Two of these boys are wearing exactly the same PE kit.
Can you spot which ones they are?

Sport-doku

A football, a hockey stick, a
tennis racket, a rounders bat
– the perfect ingredients for
an awesome PE lesson.

Fill in the blank boxes to
complete the grid. Each row,
each column and each mini
grid must have only one of
each item.

Bad Sportsmanship

Can you spot ten differences between these two pictures of how not to behave in a PE lesson? Quickly ... before someone gets hurt!

AND YOU THINK YOUR SCHOOL LESSONS ARE TOUGH!

Imagine you live in a small English village nearly two thousand years ago, working on your family's farm. Life is hard but happy. Until one day ...

The Roman Army has invaded and you are taken to Rome as a slave. You're sent to Gladiator School to train as a 'Bestiarii' - a gladiator who fights animals, such as lions, tigers, bears and alligators, to entertain the crowds.

You are led to a dark cell where you lie down on the cold stone floor and try to sleep. Early next morning you are taken to the training field.

At first, you attack a pole with wooden weapons. You're the new boy and won't be allowed real weapons until you've gone through an intense fitness regime and many practice fights. Your training weapon is much heavier than a real one, to build up your strength. After a few minutes, your arms are very tired, but you must continue, or be punished.

Next, you have to strike a shield. The first blow hits the target, making the apparatus spin, and a large wooden arm carrying a heavy sandbag strikes your head. You fall to the ground, while the trainer laughs. You quickly learn that fighting is about dodging blows as much as striking them.

This is your life now. All day, every day, you learn how to use your weapons. When you find out that all you'll have to protect yourself during a fight is your spear, you train even harder!

Your training finally complete, you are taken to a huge stadium in the centre of Rome - the Colosseum! Thousands of people have come to watch.

After waiting in a small cell underneath the seats, you finally walk out into the huge, circular arena. Seconds later, a cage door opens on the far side of the arena and a large lion appears. It roars fiercely and races straight towards you. This is it, the moment you've been training for! You grip your spear tightly and step forward ...

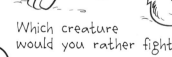

Which creature would you rather fight?

Draw yourself as a gladiator
ready to entertain the crowds.

THE ART OF SCIENCE

It's not only chefs who need to know about ingredients. Scientists know that most things are made up of a mixture of several different substances.

Release A Rainbow

This experiment will show you all the different colours that go into making one felt-tip pen colour.

You Will Need:
- Felt-tip pens • Scissors
- Kitchen roll • A water glass
- Water • Sticky tape
- A clean, dry tea towel.

Method Mayhem

1. Cut a sheet of kitchen roll long enough to fit around the inside of the glass (about 25 centimetres).

2. Use your felt-tip pens to draw four circles on the paper 5 centimetres from one of the edges, and colour them in. These circles should be about 2 centimetres across. You can use any colours you wish, but make sure each of the circles is a different colour.

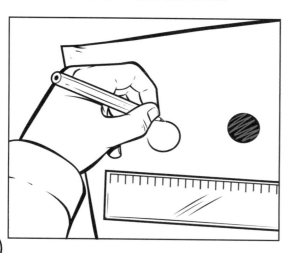

3. Pour water into the glass to a depth of 2 centimetres.

4. Roll the paper into a tube just big enough to fit inside the glass. The paper should be positioned so that the water reaches the bottom of the paper, but not the felt-tip pen circles.

5. Leave for about 30 minutes to give the water time to travel up the paper.

6. Remove the paper from the glass and leave it on the tea towel to dry.

7. Once the paper is dry, take a close look at it. Jot down what you can see and answer the questions on the opposite page.

8. Use a pair of scissors to cut out the colour that has separated the most and stick it in the space on the opposite page using sticky tape.

Stick Your Paper Here

Real Results

When you look at the paper after the experiment, you will see that each circle has travelled up the paper and separated into different colours.

1. Which colour felt-tip separated into the most colours?

....

2. Which colour travelled the furthest up the sheet of kitchen paper?

....

3. Did any of the colours surprise you?

....

Any other observations:

....

....

Cool Conclusion

Ink separates in this way because each colour is made by mixing different coloured dyes together. These dyes all have different weights. The water carries the lighter dyes further up the paper.

Fantastic Fact

Separating mixtures like this is called 'chromatography'.

MAKING TIME FLY

If you have a few minutes to spare between lessons,
why not make your very own jet fighter?
All you need is a piece of A4 paper.

1. First, fold the paper in half
lengthways and then open it out again.

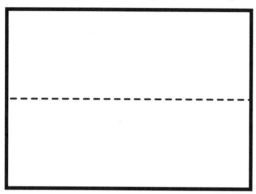

2. Next, fold a triangle from
one side into the middle fold.

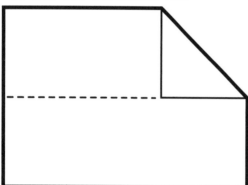

3. Then, fold another triangle into
the middle fold from the other side.

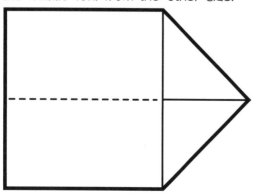

4. Now, fold one of the sides
over to the centre fold again.

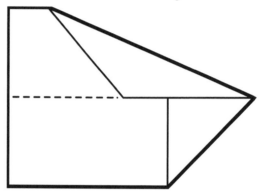

5. Do the same on the other side.

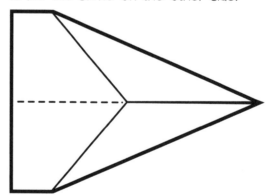

6. Fold the plane in half along
the middle fold, so the other
folds are on the inside.

7. Next, fold one side down, to make one of the wings.

8. Finally, do the same with the other side. Your jet fighter is now ready to fly!

Plane Puzzle

Which boy flew which paper plane? Find out on page 62.

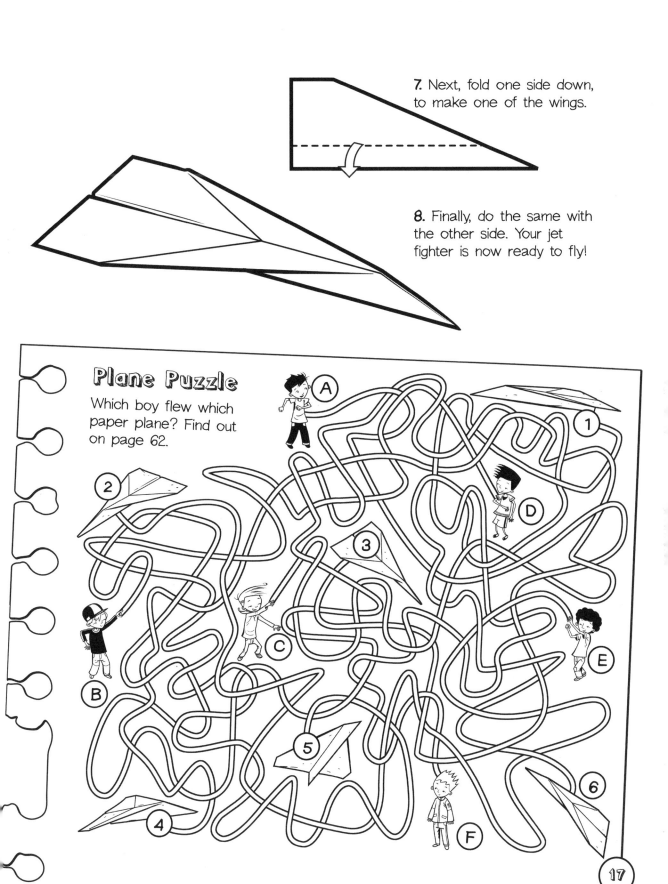

BEAT THIS!

When it comes to music, nothing beats playing along to all your favourite tracks with your very own drum kit. You can make one by following these simple steps.

You Will Need:
- Containers - metal bowls, biscuit tins and cake tins all make good drums • Sticky tape
- Scissors • Plastic wrap • Hairdryer
- Two sticks to use for drumming - you could try wooden spoons.

1. For each container, cut two pieces of plastic wrap large enough to go right over the top and a few centimetres down the sides.

2. Tape both pieces of plastic wrap over the top of the container. Do this by using the sticky tape all the way around, about 5 centimetres from the top.

3. Once an adult has shown you how to use the hairdryer, blow hot air over the plastic wrap. This will shrink it and make the drum-skin very tight.

You have now made your first drum! Repeat the process with the other containers to make a whole kit. If you want, you can include one or two tin lids as cymbals. Finally, pick up your drumsticks and **MAKE SOME NOISE!**

If you had a band, what would it be called? Write the name here ...

- - - - - - - - - - - - - - -

Top Tip!
Ask your parents before you do this. You could even get them to help, as two pairs of hands will make it much easier. Don't hold the hairdryer too close to the plastic wrap or it'll melt!

ROCK 'N' WRONG

The school band is blasting out some cool tunes. Unfortunately, there are eight things wrong with the picture below. Colour a drum in the panel each time you spot a mistake and check your answers on page 62.

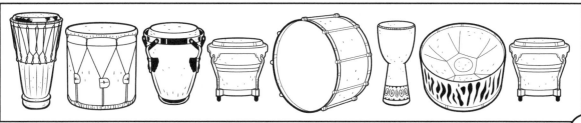

PUZZLE PUPIL

Make sure you are top of the class when it comes to solving puzzles.
Check all your answers on page 62.

The School Photo

Can you spot the ten differences between the two photos below?

Visit Your School Friend

You're off to visit your new school friend, but you're not quite sure which house is his. See if you can correctly identify your friend's house using his instructions below.

- Your friend couldn't remember his house number, but he knows it is an even number.

- He says there is a big tree in the back garden.

- There is a house on either side of your friend's house.

- You know it isn't opposite Number 9, because that is where your grandparents live.

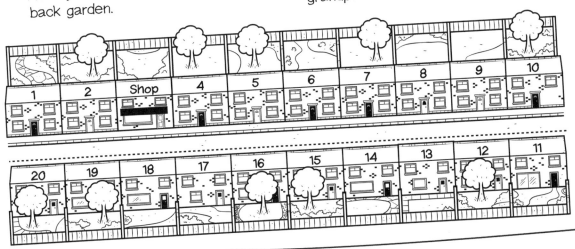

Reach The Classroom

Tim needs your help to get to his classroom. To get there, he has to cross the playground without stepping on an even number or any number that can be divided by 3.

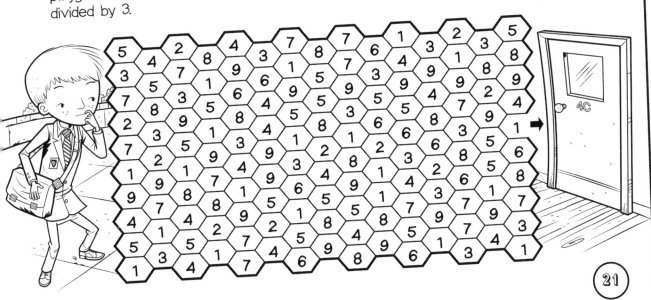

21

DESK FOOTBALL

Believe it or not, you don't need a pitch or a ball to play football. You can have an exciting match with just three coins and a couple of rulers. Here's how.

You Will Need:
- Desk or table
- Sticky tape or chalk
- 2 rulers
- 3 coins.

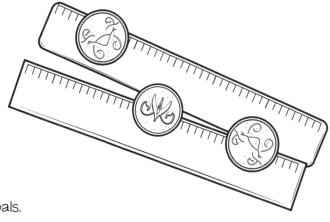

1. Use chalk or sticky tape to mark a goal (about 15 centimetres wide) at each end of a desk. You should also mark the halfway line between the goals.

2. Put three coins in a line at one end of the desk. The coin in the middle should be a different size or colour from the other two. This is your scoring coin.

4. Next, flick one of the other coins through the gap that has been made. Continue working your way up the desk by flicking each coin in turn between the other two.

Rule: You are not allowed to move backwards.

3. Flick the middle coin forward with your ruler. You must flick the coin - if you push it, this is a foul and it is the other player's turn.

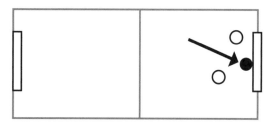

5. Once the scoring coin is over the halfway line, you can shoot for goal whenever you're ready.

6. The other player then lines the three coins up at his end of the desk. It is his turn to work his way up the desk by flicking the coins.

The first player to score three goals is the winner!

Fouls

If you commit any of the following fouls, remove your coins and it is the other player's turn:

- The coin does not pass through the other two.
- The coin hits another coin.
- The coin falls off the edge of the desk.

Copy Kit

Which football kit matches the boy's? Check your answer on page 62.

A

B

C

D

TIME TO SHAPE UP

The two brain-busting shape puzzles below will really put you to the test. You can check to see if you were correct on page 62.

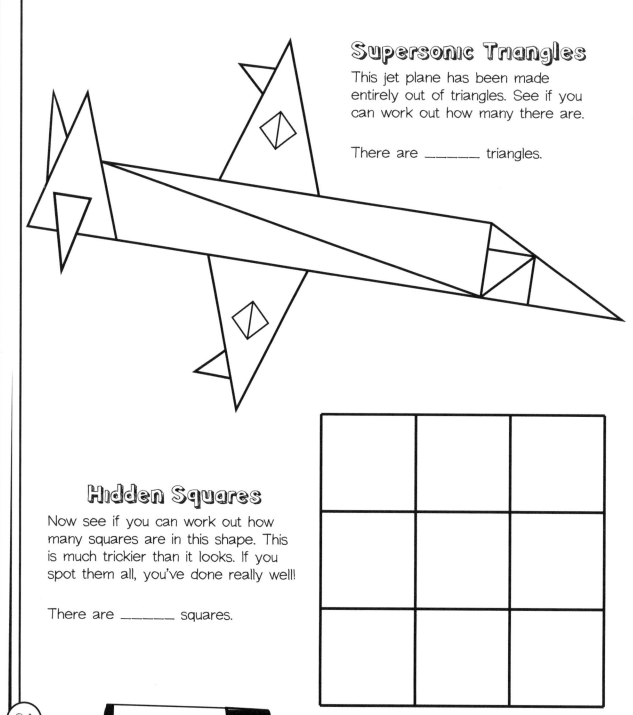

Supersonic Triangles

This jet plane has been made entirely out of triangles. See if you can work out how many there are.

There are _____ triangles.

Hidden Squares

Now see if you can work out how many squares are in this shape. This is much trickier than it looks. If you spot them all, you've done really well!

There are _____ squares.

SSSSNAKE CHALLENGE

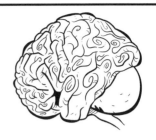

Here's a challenge to test your motor skills as well as your brain's power to adapt. You will need the snake picture below, a mirror and a pencil.

Stand in front of a mirror with the book open at this page, resting on your chest just below your chin. Do not look down at the book. You should see the page in the mirror only.

1. Place your pencil at the base of the snake's head.

2. Now move your pencil so that you draw a line all the way to the snake's tail. You have to stay within the snake.

You might find this exercise much harder than you think, because the mirror image confuses your brain.

CALLING PLANET EARTH

How well do you know your own home, planet Earth? Have a competition with your friends and mark each player's answers (A, B, C or D) on the scorecard on page 27. Then check your answers on page 62.

1. Which is the world's biggest ocean?

A. The Pacific Ocean
B. The Atlantic Ocean
C. The Indian Ocean
D. The Arctic Ocean

2. Where is the Amazon Rainforest?

A. Asia
B. Europe
C. South America
D. North America

3. Which country has the largest population?

A. The United States
B. Russia
C. India
D. China

4. Why are there no fish in the Dead Sea in the Middle East?

A. There is no water in this sea
B. The water is too salty
C. The sharks eat them all
D. They have all been caught

5. The equator is an imaginary line that ...

A. Runs around the middle of the Earth
B. Joins the North and South Pole
C. Joins London to New York
D. Joins the Earth to the moon

6. How many continents are there?

A. 6
B. 7
C. 8
D. 10

7. Which of these is not an island?

A. Jamaica
B. France
C. Japan
D. New Zealand

8. What type of weather is likely in a monsoon?

A. Ice
B. Drought
C. Rain
D. Fog

9. Which is the world's highest mountain?

A. Mount Kilimanjaro
B. Mont Blanc
C. Mount St Helens
D. Mount Everest

11. Which of these rivers flows through India?

A. The Ganges
B. The Nile
C. The Mississippi
D. The Thames

10. Which sea lies between Europe and Africa?

A. The North Sea
B. The Baltic Sea
C. The Mediterranean Sea
D. The Caribbean Sea

12. Which of these is the odd one out?

A. Texas
B. Florida
C. California
D. Canada

Question	Player 1	Player 2	Player 3	Player 4
1				
2				
3				
4				
5				
6				
7				
8				
9				
10				
11				
12				
Total				

INCREDIBLE BOUNCING EGGS

You Will Need:
- A hard-boiled egg
- Vinegar - any kind will do, but white vinegar will make it easier to see what's going on
- An old glass jar.

What To Do:

1. Ask an adult to hard boil an egg for you. Then, once it's cool enough to touch, place the egg in the jar and pour in enough vinegar to cover it.

2. After a few minutes, you'll start to notice a few changes. Tiny bubbles will start to appear all over the shell and it may start to spin in the vinegar!

3. Wait half an hour and then gently rub the shell with your finger - it should start to come off quite easily. Then put the egg back.

4. You'll need to leave the egg for three days to get the bounciest results. Put the jar in an out-of-the-way place, where it won't get knocked over.

5. After three days in the vinegar, rinse any remaining shell off the egg under running water. You'll be left with a rubbery, bouncy, unpredictable eggy toy!

Science Stuff

Eggshell is made of a substance called calcium carbonate. The acid in the vinegar eats away at it and leaves the egg inside rubbery at the same time.

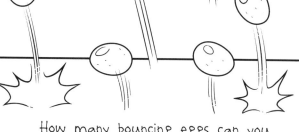

How many bouncing eggs can you count? Check the number on page 62.

AN EGG-CELLENT TRICK

Try standing a raw egg on its end so that it stands up. You'll quickly find that it's impossible! Here's how to amaze your friends with your egg-balancing powers.

1. First, take a little bit of fine salt and make a small mound on the table.

2. Carefully balance a raw egg on the mound of salt.

3. Once you've done this, gently blow the mound of salt away.

When they come to look, all your friends will see is an egg standing upright. Now challenge them to do the same - without telling them about the salt, of course!

Add a funny face to this egg.

PUZZLE PLANET

Does the globe have you in a spin? Solve these
puzzles and check your answers on page 63.

Where In The World?

Match the names of the countries to their shapes.
The UK has already been matched to start you off.

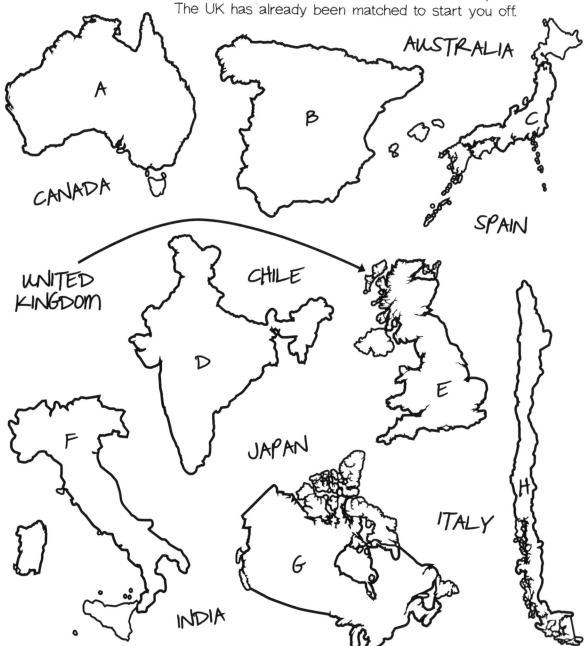

AUSTRALIA

CANADA

SPAIN

UNITED
KINGDOM

CHILE

JAPAN

ITALY

INDIA

A

B

C

D

E

F

G

H

That Looks Familiar

See if you can link each famous landmark to the country where
it's located and to the correct picture. The first one has been done for you.

STONEHENGE

THE SYDNEY
OPERA HOUSE

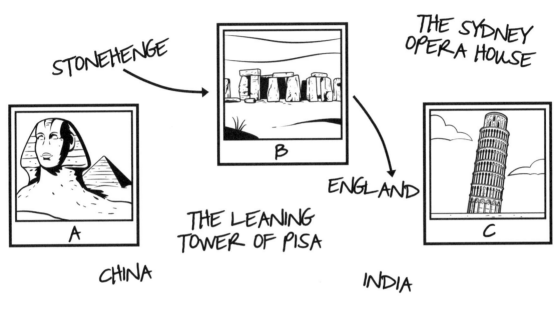

ENGLAND

THE LEANING
TOWER OF PISA

CHINA

INDIA

THE STATUE OF
LIBERTY

AUSTRALIA

EGYPT

USA

THE TAJ MAHAL

THE GREAT
WALL

ITALY

THE SPHINX

A BUG'S LIFE

How good are you at bug spotting? It's time to find out!
Check your answers on page 63.

Shadow Shapes

The six insects below are an ant, a grasshopper,
a ladybird, a beetle, a spider and a caterpillar.
Decide which insect is which.

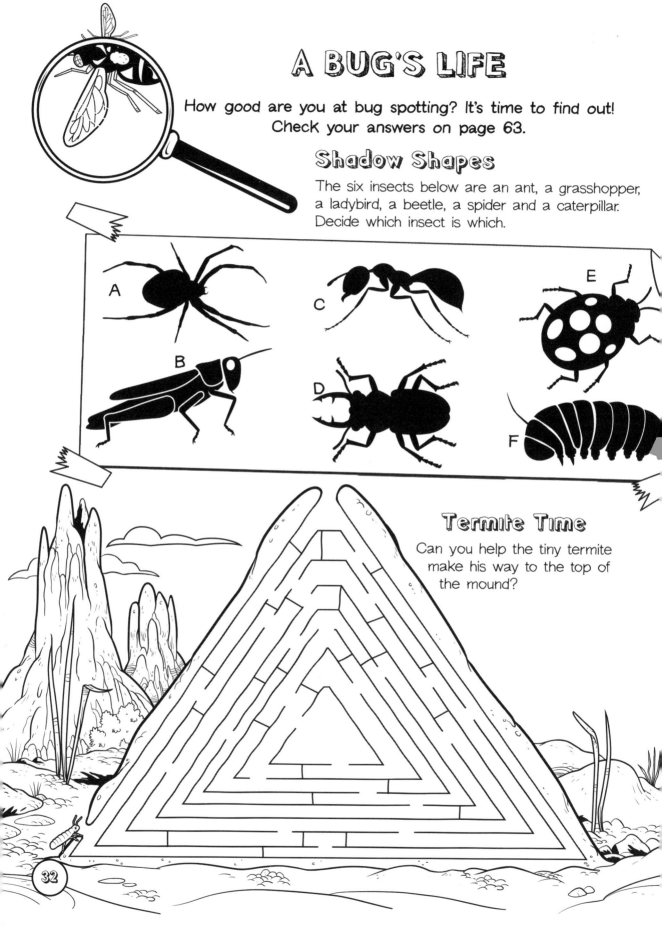

A

B

C

D

E

F

Termite Time

Can you help the tiny termite
make his way to the top of
the mound?

Spot The Stick Insects

Many insects can be pretty hard to spot, but the most difficult to find is the stick insect. This is because it really does look like a stick! Can you spot ten in the scene below?

More About Stick Insects

Their scientific name is Phasmatodea. This comes from the Ancient Greek word 'phasma', meaning phantom.

They are known as walking sticks or stick-bugs in the United States and Canada, and as phasmids, ghost insects and leaf insects in other places.

A SAFE PLACE?

Here's a spooky story for you to scare your friends with on a school trip.

The branch gave a loud crack and Billy slipped even lower. He looked into the swirling fog and began to panic. He had no idea how far down the ground was.

It was the last day of the school trip to the Outdoors Centre, and Billy had gone for an early morning walk before the coach came to take everybody home. The sky had been clear when he set off, but the fog came down quickly.

He soon became lost and walked straight off the top of the cliff without seeing the edge. He only just managed to grab hold of the branch to stop himself plunging to the bottom!

CRACK! The branch bent lower still. Billy felt his hands slipping and knew he couldn't hold on much longer. CRACK! To Billy's horror, the branch snapped off the tree completely.

Everything seemed to happen in slow motion. As he fell, he felt a strong hand grab his and found himself dangling in mid air. Looking up, he saw two piercing blue eyes shining through the fog, as a white-haired old man leaned over the cliff edge with his arm outstretched.

Billy felt himself being pulled upwards and was surprised at the strength in the old man's arm. Reaching the top of the cliff, he sank down on to the grass. When he looked up, the old man had gone, silently disappearing into the fog.

Billy ran to the Centre and was relieved to be back with his classmates. As they waited for the coach, Billy noticed a big painting behind the reception desk of a man he recognized. "Excuse me. Who's the man in the painting?" he asked the manager.

"That's my father," replied the manager. "He built this place."

"Can I meet him? I'd like to say thanks."

"I wish you could. Unfortunately, he died years ago." The manager smiled, sadly. "He loved this place. He was proud to provide a safe place for children to have fun. In all the years we've been open, there hasn't been one accident."

A horn sounded. "Sounds as if your coach is here. Time to go, I'm afraid."

"I guess he's still looking after the place," Billy thought to himself.

· Mr. H. Simmons ·

Draw a picture of the mysterious
old man with piercing blue eyes.

WHERE DID I LEAVE MY SOCKS?

It's your first day back at school and you need to find your uniform.
Unfortunately, you forgot to tidy your bedroom during the holidays!

You only have ten minutes to get ready before you have to leave and you need to find the following ten items in your room. Circle them when you spot them and, if you get stuck, turn to page 63.

- Two socks
- Two shoes
- A pair of trousers
- A rucksack
- A shirt
- A tie
- A hooded coat
- A jumper

SORRY I'M LATE, MISS!

Only one of the four cycle paths below will take you from your home to school. Unless you find it, you are going to be late for your first lesson! The right route is revealed on page 63.

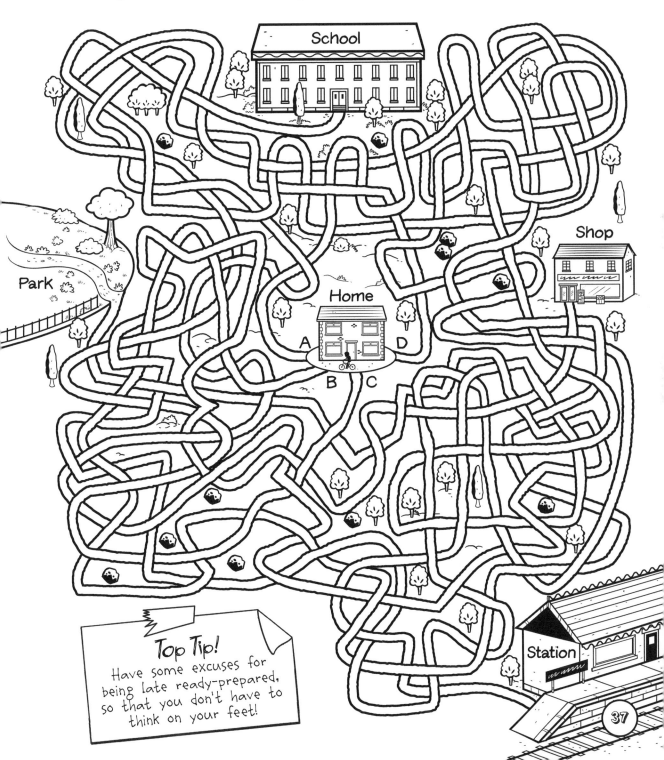

School

Park

Shop

Home

A   D

B   C

Station

Top Tip!
Have some excuses for being late ready-prepared, so that you don't have to think on your feet!

CLASSROOM CONFUSION

There's chaos in the classroom. Solve the puzzles and check your answers on pages 63 and 64.

What's Wrong?

There are eight mistakes for you to spot in this picture of a maths lesson.

Calculations On The Clock

Time yourself to see how quickly you can solve these sums. Write your time here:

_____

9 - 7 =

8 + 9 =

4 + 5 =

15 ÷ 3 =

12 ÷ 4 =

7 x 5 =

6 x 3 =

13 - 6 =

14 ÷ 7 =

Oops! I've Lost My Classroom

It's your first day back at school and you're told that, this year, you will be taught in classroom B6. Unfortunately, you don't know where it is!

You ask some of your friends and they give you the information below. Use it to decide which classroom you need to go to, then double-check on page 64.

- John tells you: "It's one of the classrooms next to the playground."

- Tom says: "It's on the same corridor as the Science Lab."

- Eric adds: "It's not one of the rooms next to the Staff Room."

- Finally, Alex says: "It's not the classroom opposite the Library."

Classroom	Classroom	Science Lab		Classroom	Classroom

Corridor

Storeroom	Classroom	Classroom	Staffroom	Classroom	Classroom	Library

Classroom	Classroom	Playground	Classroom	Classroom

Corridor   Corridor

WONDER DOGS!

In history lessons, you will learn about many famous heroes. What may surprise you, though, is that some of the world's greatest heroes were actually dogs! Here are the stories of three of them.

Pickles

Football's World Cup is the world's most famous sporting trophy. In 1966, the contest was to be held in England but, shortly before it started, the trophy was stolen! Over a hundred detectives searched frantically while the whole world watched and waited. Despite their efforts, the trophy couldn't be found.

A week after the theft, Pickles, a black and white mongrel, was out walking with his owner when his attention was caught by something hidden under a hedge. It was the famous trophy everyone had been searching for! The country was overjoyed, and Pickles became a national hero. He was a guest of honour at the England team's banquet after they won the trophy, receiving a standing ovation. He was even allowed to lick all the plates clean!

Gandalf

Twelve-year-old Michael Auberry was on a camping trip with his scout troop when he wandered off and became lost in the mountains of North Carolina in the USA. Hundreds of volunteers searched for him, while heat-seeking helicopters flew overhead.

The days passed, and people grew more and more worried. Meanwhile, Michael was lost, hungry and thirsty. He saw the helicopters above and heard the search parties, but no one heard when he called.

Luckily, among those searching was Misha Marshall and her Shiloh Shepherd dog, Gandalf. The dog sniffed around and picked up the boy's scent close to the campsite. Following it, he led the rescuers to a very relieved Michael.

Nome And The Sled Dogs

The doctor in the small Alaskan town of Nome was worried when locals started falling sick. He recognized the signs of diphtheria – a contagious bacterial infection that mainly affects the nose and throat – and knew the disease would spread very quickly through the entire population. He needed medicine fast, but the nearest serum was 1,000 kilometres (621 miles) away!

In a race against time, 150 sled dogs raced in teams across the frozen Alaskan wilderness to fetch the medicine.

Early one morning, the doctor heard a knock on his door. Opening it, he was handed a bag of serum by the sled driver, a team of exhausted sled dogs behind him. Each dog was a true hero and a statue of the final team's lead dog, Balto, can be seen in New York's Central Park.

Design a medal of honour to be awarded to heroic dogs.

SSSH ... A MATHS SHORT CUT

The 9 timestable can be quite tricky, but by using this simple method, you'll never have trouble with it again.

All you need to do is hold your hands out in front of you with your palms facing you, and then ...

1 x 9
Bend finger 1 (the thumb on the left hand). There are 0 fingers on the left of this finger (the tens column) and 9 fingers to the right of this finger (the units column), so the answer is 9.

2 x 9
Bend finger 2. There is 1 finger to the left (making 1 in the tens column) and 8 fingers to the right (making 8 in the units column), so the answer is 18.

You can then follow the same pattern for the rest of the 9 timestable!

What's 7x9?

The answer is 63!

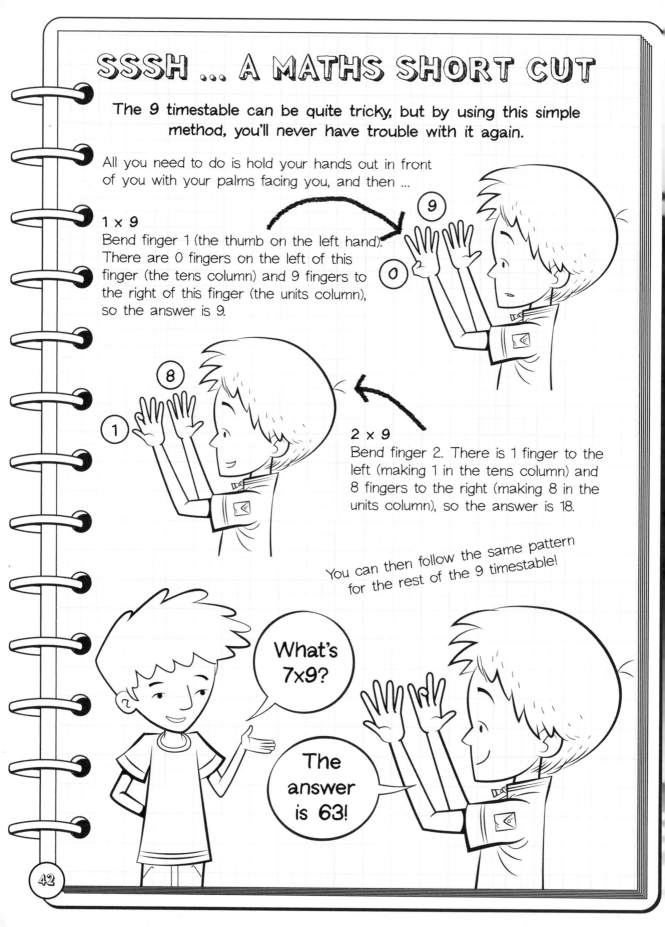

CROSS NUMBERS!

This maths teacher has a challenge for you! Can you fill in the white squares in the grid below by reading the clues and working out the correct answers? The first one has been done for you and you can check the other answers on page 64.

Across

- c. 2 x 11
- e. 70 − 7
- g. 40 + 4
- j. 125 − 5
- k. Half of 1,000
- l. 129 x 4
- n. Two thousand, three hundred and sixty-seven
- p. Twice as much as 500
- q. 2 x 80

Down

- a. A dozen
- b. 3 x 12
- d. Twice as much as 100
- f. 40 − 6
- h. 5 x 9
- i. 1,000 x 2 + 7
- j. Half of 310
- m. 52 + 9
- n. 5 + 5 + 5 + 5
- o. Four less than 700

A STRANGE WAY
TO LOOK AT STUFF

The pictures on this page are shown from a very unusual angle. See if you can work out what they are, then check if you were right on page 64.

A

C

B

D

44

YOUR VERY OWN TOTEM POLE

Complete this totem pole as a symbol for your tribe.

Some Native American tribes made huge wooden sculptures, known as totem poles. They display symbols for families and tribes, and include faces, birds, snakes and mythical creatures.

Top Tip!
This totem pole shape makes a great bookmark. Why not cut the shape out, stick it on to a piece of card, and then decorate it as colourfully as you can?

SCHOOL STATUE

Every school needs a statue. Design one for your school here.

CAN YOU KEEP A SECRET?

Use this page to create a secret language for you and your school friends, then you can have a good chat without anybody else knowing what you are talking about! Once you've invented your code words, swear your friends to secrecy and then let them make a copy.

The code words can be real or invented. For example, 'really good' could be a word such as 'smooth', or something you have made up such as 'dreppy'.

TOP SECRET

Word	Code Word	Word	Code Word
School		School bag	
Food		Funny	
Book		Really good	
Friend		Computer	
Playground			
Teacher			
Girl			
Boy			
Lunch			
Sweets			
Football			
Boring			

Add more words that you'll find useful.

BOY GENIUS

Wolfgang Amadeus Mozart is one of the most famous musicians of all time. Born in Austria in 1756, he composed over 50 symphonies and his music is still loved today.

At just three years old, long before children even start school, he could play a musical instrument called the clavier, a type of keyboard.

When he was four, his father, Leopold, gave Mozart's older sister a piece of music to practise. Mozart could play it in less than half an hour!

Mozart was composing his own music when he was five and, within another year, he was performing concerts in Austria, touring Europe and playing in Germany, France and England.

By the age of eight, he had composed three complete symphonies, and at age 12, he had written two operas.

It is said that Mozart was so good that he could pick up an instrument and play it without a single lesson, and he could write down all the notes to a piece of music after hearing it just once.

Which sheet of music matches Mozart's?
Make sure you're right by turning to page 64.

INVASION OF THE MARTIANS

You've written a thrilling story about Earth being attacked by an alien invasion force. It's so good, the teacher wants to put it in the school library so everyone can read it! So, you need to design a really exciting front cover to make your book stand out from all the others.

SUPER-STRONG FRIENDS

Follow these instructions to show four of your friends how strong they actually are. They'll be amazed by their superhuman strength.

Here's how four friends can lift you up using just their fingers. Sit on a chair without arms and stay very still.

Two of your friends should stand behind the chair, the third should stand at the right-hand side of the chair and the fourth at the left-hand side.

Ask one of your friends to place his left hand on top of your head. Your three other friends should then place their left hands on top of his. Ask them to do the same with their right hands, so all eight hands are on your head.

The four lifters must really concentrate now. They should all chant, 'Light as a feather! Stiff as a board!' 20 times, whilst thinking hard about raising you up into the air.

The lifters should then remove their hands and each press their left and right hands together, with both their index fingers sticking out and the others clasped round each other.

The two friends at either side of the chair should put these two fingers under each of your knees. The two friends standing behind the chair should place their fingers under your armpits.

Now, count to three out loud. When you call out 'three', everybody should

lift upwards with their fingers and you will lift up, as if you really were as light as a feather! Your friends should be able to lift you quite high, but make sure they let you down again carefully and gently.

Top Tip!
It can take two or three goes to get this to work properly. If it does not work first time, remember to start again from the beginning and repeat the chanting.

WHAT'S MISSING?

It's time to test your friends' powers of observation.

Collect ten objects and place them on a table. You can use any objects lying around the classroom, such as a pencil, a text book, a paintbrush, a calculator, a coin, a pen, a ruler, an eraser, an apple and a cup.

Give a friend 60 seconds to look at the objects, then send him out of the room.

While he is outside, quickly remove and hide one of the objects and then shuffle the other objects around a bit.

When your friend comes back into the classroom, he has to tell you which object is now missing.

As an alternative, you could ask your friends to look at the objects shown above for 60 seconds. Then cover them up and see how many your friends can remember.

Friend 1 remembered _____ objects.

Friend 2 remembered _____ objects.

Friend 3 remembered _____ objects.

AMAZING ANIMAL FACTS

Science fiction writers have dreamt up some really strange aliens to scare us. However, nothing in their imagination is as strange or scary as some creatures already on our planet!

Rhinoceros Beetle

Ask people to name the strongest animal in the world and they will probably say "elephant". However, the tiny rhinoceros beetle is so strong it can lift up to 850 times its own weight. That's the same as one man lifting up nine fully-grown male African elephants!

Tarantula

These spiders have large, hairy bodies. Many people are scared of them, but they look more threatening than they actually are. The venom from their bite is mild, weaker than a bee's in fact. South America is home to some of the biggest types of tarantula, such as the Goliath spider, with a leg span of up to 30 centimetres.

Shark

If your boat sinks in shark-infested waters, you've got problems if you cut yourself, because a shark can smell a single drop of blood in a million drops of seawater. They also have an endless supply of teeth to replace ones that fall out. One shark may grow and shed up to 50,000 teeth in its lifetime.

Praying Mantis

The praying mantis can turn its head all the way around and back to where it started from. Scary!

Add your own amazing animal fact here.

OCTOPROF

What do you get when you cross a teacher with an octopus?
Draw your answer below.

A LOGICAL SOLUTION

Can you complete these three logic challenges? You're allowed five minutes for each challenge. You can find the solutions on page 64.

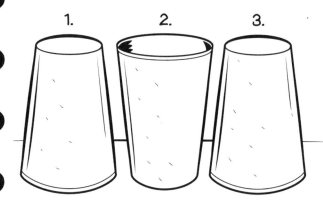

1.   2.   3.

Three Cups

Line three paper cups up, so that the middle one is the right way up and the other two are upside down.

Now, you have to get all the cups the right way up by turning over two cups at a time. It's easy to do it in one move or two moves, but can you do it in exactly three moves?

Feeding Time

You have a weekend job feeding the animals at the zoo. You have to feed them in the right order. Can you work this out from the three clues?

- The wolves are fed before the zebras, but after the monkeys.
- The penguins are fed straight after the monkeys.
- The tigers are fed straight after the zebras.

Feeding Schedule	
1st	
2nd	
3rd	
4th	
5th	

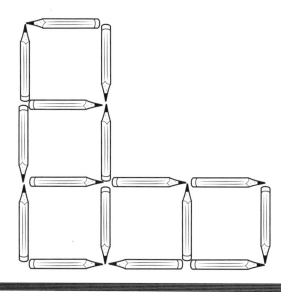

Moving Squares

By moving just two pencils, change this shape into four complete squares of the same size.

MORE STRANGE VIEWS

Here are some more pictures from unusual angles. Check to see if you guessed them all correctly on page 64.

PLAYGROUND FUN

The best thing about school is the fun you can have playing games at break time. Here are a couple of great games to try. Both of them will test your shooting marksmanship.

Bullseye

Collect a few pebbles and a piece of chalk and then challenge your friends to a game of Bullseye. The first thing to do is to make your target:

- Draw a circle on the ground, about 50 centimetres wide.
- Draw a second circle around the first, about 30 centimetres away from the first circle.

- Draw a third, fourth and fifth circle, leaving a space of 30 centimetres each time.
- Write the number 10 in the smallest circle.
- Write 5 in the second smallest circle, 3 in the third circle, 2 in the fourth circle and 1 in the biggest circle.

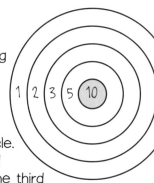

Once you've made your target, draw a line about 3 metres away. Player 1 stands on the line and throws a stone at the smallest circle. This is the bullseye. If he lands in it, he scores 10 points. If he lands in one of the larger circles, he scores 5, 3, 2, or 1 points. If the pebble lands on a line between two circles, the higher score counts.

The next player then has a throw. Each player throws three stones. The one with the highest number of points after three throws is the winner!

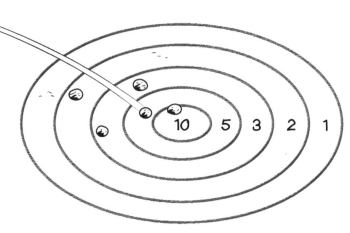

Sock-Ball Tag

You probably already know how to play Tag. It's the game where you have to run after and touch the other players.

Sock-Ball Tag is slightly different, because the player doing the chasing has to use a sock ball to catch the other players.

Making a sock ball is very simple. You just roll up a pair of old socks!

The player who is the thrower chases after the other players and throws the sock ball at his chosen target. If he hits the person, that player is the one who then has to do the chasing.

How many pencils can you spot hidden in the scene?

Answers on page 64.

THINGS BEGINNING WITH ...

It's time to test your general knowledge! Compete against three friends to see who can score the most points in this alphabet game. First, each player must make a grid like the one shown here.

One player then chooses a letter and all the players try to fill in their grids with words beginning with that letter, Keep your grids a secret! When every player has finished, score your answers in each column like this:

- For an answer that no-one else has: 2 points.
- For an answer that another player also has: 1 point.
- No answer: 0 points.

The next player then chooses a letter and another round is played. The winner is the player with the most points in total at the end of six rounds.

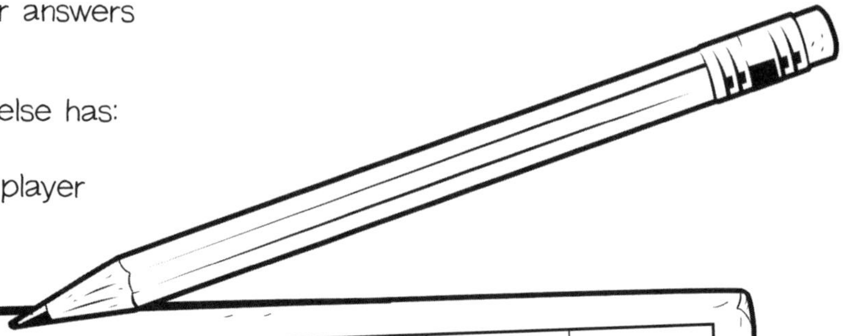

Round	Letter	Country	Film or TV character	Food	Sport or game	Boy's name	Total points
1	B	Bolivia 2	Batman 1	Bread 1	Boxing 1	Ben 2	7
2							
3							
4							
5							
6							

Above is an example of how you could fill out your grid for the letter B. This player named a country and a boy's name that no-one else thought of and had answers for the other questions that were the same as other players, so he scores 7 points for that round.

WHICH WARRIOR IS WHICH?

Can you name the warriors in the pictures? The Roman Soldier has been done to start you off! The correct answers are on page 64.

World War II Soldier

American Civil War Soldier

Jousting Knight

Native American Brave

Roman Soldier

Crusader

Samurai Warrior

Viking Warrior

MAKE A SUSPENSION BRIDGE

Suspension bridges are held up by thick cables, making them very strong indeed. To see how they work, why not make your own suspension bridge and carry out a simple strength test?

1. First, build a normal bridge. To do this, make one of the bridge towers by taping two straws together at the top. Cut a small piece of straw and tape this between the two straws. Make a second tower in the same way.

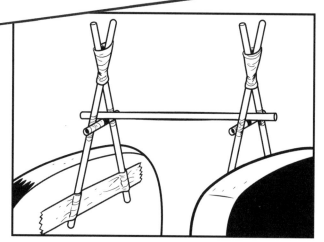

2. Place another straw between the two towers, with each end resting on the cross-piece of the towers. Then put two chairs close together and tape a tower to each chair.

3. Poke two holes in a paper cup and tie one end of a length of string to each hole.

4. Lift up the straw between the towers and slide the string over it. Put some stones in the cup, one at a time, until the straw in the middle bends. Make a note of the number of stones you have used.

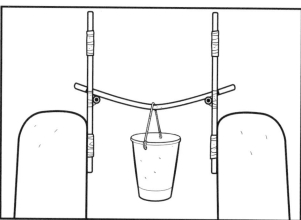

5. Now, turn the normal bridge into a suspension bridge. Remove the cup and use a new straw to replace the bent one. Tie some string around the middle of the new straw and then place one end of the string over the top of each tower. Pull each end down the other side until tight and tape them down.

See how many stones the bridge will now hold. This will show you how much stronger a suspension bridge is compared with a normal bridge.

Results Table

	Normal bridge	Suspension bridge
Number of stones		

ALL THE ANSWERS

ARE YOU THE HISTORY KING?
Pages 6 and 7

1. B	4. D	7. B	10. D
2. A	5. C	8. B	11. D
3. A	6. A	9. C	12. C

EXTREME SPORTS LESSON
Pages 10 and 11

Get Ready For Games:
Boys B and E are wearing the same kit.

Sport-doku:

Bad Sportsmanship:

PLANE PUZZLE
Page 17

A. 3	C. 4	E. 2
B. 6	D. 5	F. 1

ROCK 'N' WRONG
Page 19

PUZZLE PUPIL
Pages 20 and 21

The School Photo:

Visit Your School Friend:
Your friend lives in house number 16.

Reach The Classroom:

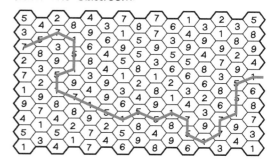

COPY KIT
Page 23

Football kit C.

TIME TO SHAPE UP
Page 24

Supersonic Triangles:
There are 20 triangles.

Hidden Squares:
There are 14 squares.

CALLING PLANET EARTH
Pages 26 and 27

1. A	4. B	7. B	10. C
2. C	5. A	8. C	11. A
3. D	6. B	9. D	12. D

INCREDIBLE BOUNCING EGGS
Page 28

There are 18 bouncing eggs.

PUZZLE PLANET
Pages 30 and 31

Where In The World?:

A. Australia
B. Spain
C. Japan
D. India
E. United Kingdom
F. Italy
G. Canada
H. Chile

That Looks Familiar:

A. The Sphinx, Egypt.
B. Stonehenge, England.
C. The Leaning Tower of Pisa, Italy.
D. The Statue of Liberty, USA.
E. The Sydney Opera House, Australia.
F. The Great Wall, China.
G. The Taj Mahal, India.

A BUG'S LIFE
Pages 32 and 33

Shadow Shapes:

A. Spider
B. Grasshopper
C. Ant
D. Beetle
E. Ladybird
F. Caterpillar

Termite Time:

Spot The Stick Insects:

WHERE DID I LEAVE MY SOCKS?
Page 36

SORRY I'M LATE, MISS!
Page 37

Take cycle path B.

CLASSROOM CONFUSION
Pages 38 and 39

What's Wrong?:

Calculations On The Clock:

9 - 7 = 2
15 ÷ 3 = 5
6 x 3 = 18
8 + 9 = 17
12 ÷ 4 = 3

13 - 6 = 7
4 + 5 = 9
7 x 5 = 35
14 ÷ 7 = 2

Oops! I've Lost My Classroom:

Classroom	Classroom	Science Lab	Classroom	Classroom

Corridor

| Storeroom | Classroom | Classroom | Staffroom | Classroom | Classroom | Library |

| Classroom | Classroom | Playground | Classroom | Classroom |

Corridor | Corridor

CROSS NUMBERS!
Page 43

A STRANGE WAY TO LOOK AT STUFF
Page 44

A. A man in a Mexican hat frying an egg.
B. Someone on their hands and knees scrubbing the floor.
C. A giraffe walking past a window.
D. A bear climbing a tree.

BOY GENIUS
Page 48

Sheet of music C matches Mozart's.

A LOGICAL SOLUTION
Page 54

Three Cups:

Turn over cups 1 and 2; turn over cups 1 and 3; turn over cups 1 and 2.

Feeding Time:

1st - monkeys. 2nd - penguins. 3rd - wolves. 4th - zebras. 5th - tigers.

Moving Squares:

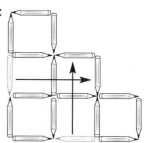

MORE STRANGE VIEWS
Page 55

A. A bald man wearing spectacles.
B. A small boy carrying a large beach ball.
C. A boy lying on top of his bed and looking underneath it.
D. A man falling down a hole.
E. A chef hiding behind a wall.
F. A man standing round a corner playing the trombone.

SOCK-BALL TAG
Page 57

There are 7 pencils in the scene.

WHICH WARRIOR IS WHICH?
Page 59

A. Viking Warrior
B. Native American Brave
C. Roman Soldier
D. Samurai Warrior
E. Crusader
F. American Civil War Soldier
G. Jousting Knight
H. World War II Soldier